# My Pathway To Spirit Communication

### A real-life beginning to
### "Proving the continuity of life"

## Linda J. Kent

To Barbara (
Lineth love + in
Happeness future.
your

Lynn Kent

My Pathway To Spirit Communication

Copyright © 2011 Linda J. Kent

ISBN 978-1-61434-493-3

Library of Congress Control Number: 2011914247

Printed in the United States of America on acid-free paper.

First Edition

Published by Kent Spiritual Publications, Seekonk, MA USA
www.kent-spiritual-publications.com
www.lynnkent.com

# Table of Contents

# About the Author

First communication with Spirit happened about 25 years ago with her departed maternal grandmother. Soon afterwards she confirmed the information she was given with her mother and aunts. From that experience she decided to learn about spirit communication and with the help of her husband, to bring this information and experience to the public.

Lynn is now an Ordained Minister and Certified Medium with the National Spiritualist Association of Churches and is on the ministerial staff with the First Spiritualist Church of Springfield Massachusetts, NSAC.

She is also National Director of the NSAC Department of Phenomenal Evidence and writes a bi-monthly report in The National Summit magazine and is past Vice President of the NSAC Ministerial and Certified Medium league.

Lynn has provided mediumship demonstration at the "ISF" International Spiritualist Federation fraternal week in Rochester New York and at the "NSAC" National Spiritualist Association of Churches convention in Portland Maine where she chaired and taught "Teach the Teachers" mediumship workshop.

She has served Spiritualist churches (as guest medium or seminar presenter) in Maine, New Hampshire, Massachusetts, Connecticut, New York, New Jersey, Virginia, Nevada, California; interviewed by ABC Channel 6, cable shows in Rhode Island and Massachusetts.

She has attended the world renowned "Arthur Finley College" in Standsted England for advanced mediumship and trance.

Before doing mediumship on a full time bases, Lynn was a hair stylist for 30 years in Bristol Rhode Island where her consoling abilities were developed. She is now using those abilities in her many pastoral counseling and spirit communication sessions, especially for children in Spirit, at her home/office in Seekonk, Massachusetts.

Lynn is a Bristol Rhode Island native and has attended local Catholic schools and considered a career as a nun. Although she changed her mind about the convent and sisterhood, she still has chosen to work with Spirit helping others in need.

Examples of her Electronic Voice Phenomena ("EVP"), Table Tipping videos and energy ORB photographs can be found on her web site along with additional background information.

# Acknowledgement and Dedication

I would like to thank all the contributions made, especially with interviews and editing by my clients, to bring the book's stories to life and their families' support for this important work. Their names and background have been changed to protect their security and privacy.

Of course very little could be accomplished without the help of my dear family and their continuance in providing a place of security and accommodation to complete this project. Especially my parents Margaret and Pasquale Mazza (dad in spirit), who raised me with love and an open mind. And to my husband who was a driving force in on my pathway to spirit.

Finally, the dedication of this material is to all those in the Spirit realm that made contact with the physical world to let everyone know there is no death and continuity of life and love is a reality.

# Preface

This is not only the beginning of a book for your reading enjoyment, but a possible whole new system of belief. It is about life after death. I am not talking about a near death experience, but a whole belief system that is rooted in something most of us have been taught not to believe in, for most of our lives. The soul or Spirit lives on after the death of the body!

As a Certified Medium I must prove this on a regular basis to those who seek knowledge and assurance that their loved-ones still exist somewhere in the Universe; their numbers are many. Most of the people I speak to are those just like you looking for confirmation that their family members are still with them. Some come to me because their own belief system does not consider the experiences they have had themselves to be real, or of a positive nature.

On television and in fiction movies and books we are shown the negative side of the "Spirit Realm". This is something most of us do not want to experience. I certainly do not! There are negative Spirits out there and I want to keep away from them. Yet there are many Spirit people wanting to get in touch with their loved ones here on earth to let them know they are okay and are still living in their own way in the Universe and with God.

My husband and I decided to write this book, with help from our Spirit relatives. There are many ways to seek out and get a good reading. Yes, a certified medium is one way; there are many of us living here in the good old USA. Yes, we have a gift, but we are trained to "prove the continuity of life". This is the basis of Spiritualism. There is a directory at the end for anyone interested in furthering his or her knowledge of Spirit.

Part of this book is a little of my story and how I got to this place, how my husband was the human enforcer that helped Spirit to give me the confidence to "go public" after serving Spiritualist churches for 9 years. I have lost many friends because of my belief system, but I have proven it over and over again that Spirit does exist and is probably standing directly behind you as you read this book.

When I say Spirit, I speak of your own dearly departed, not a stranger.

# Belief in What I Do

I Believe Communication with the "Spirit Realm"
Is a Privilege.
With this Privilege Comes Great Responsibility
I Accept this Obligation and Commitment for
Spirit Messages,
Fully Knowing that this Ability Can Influence the
Actions of Others and Their
Understanding of the Spirit World.

Reverend Linda Kent,
Certified Medium, NSAC

# Part One

# Starting My Life for Spirit

# Chapter 1
## My Beginnings

To tell you a little about my life and not bore you, I have decided to condense most of my journey to Spirit into the first few chapters. A wise man once said that the number 18 is a magical, spiritual number. With respect to this wise man I will do the same and have written 18 chapters for this book.

I came from a Catholic family; Italian on dad's side and Portuguese on mom's side. My Italian side would have a feast day called "Madonna da'Luche or Mother of the Light. " This Feast Day of Our Lady of the Light, the patron saint of my grandfather's village in Italy, was like a family reunion of the generations. It was celebrated around the middle of August each year; I always remember it being a beautiful day, and I never remember rain. The whole family would go to special mass at the Italian church in Bristol, Rhode Island, Our Lady of Mount Carmel (OLMC), one of the three Catholic churches in the small town of my birth. My paternal grandparents paid for this mass or service for this Saint. (For those who do not understand, if you wanted to have a special mass or service in the Catholic Church dedicated to a saint, loved one, or family member, you could do so for a price; this is one of the ways the individual churches support themselves.

After mass at OLMC or Mt. Carmel, as our church was known, we gathered at my grandparent's house for a feast. There must have been at least 80 of us there throughout the day. It was always the highlight of the summer and enabled me to know my relatives who had recently arrived from Italy; they always arrived later in the day for a different round of food. This scrumptious food was made in the Old Italian tradition accompanied by plenty of homemade wine. I truly loved that wonderful day in August. Knowing and understanding the new arrivals helped me to understand many of the messages I received from my grandparents later when attending Spiritualist churches in my adult life.

My maternal grandmother was a very devoted Catholic. My great aunt, my grandmother's sister, still in Portugal in 1917, was reported to be at Fatima when the Miracle of Fatima took place. You can see my Catholic roots went deep. I learned the Rosary from my "Vo-Vo" (Portuguese grandmother) as she had learned it from her mother. There is even a wonderful story related to Spirit that happened yearly when my Vo-Vo was alive and I was a child. Every year that I can remember a white dove would fly to my grandmother's window, the one she hung the clothes from after washing. The window was at the top of the stairway to the bedrooms of her house. This dove would always appear on or around the anniversary of my grandfather's death (her husband), in the middle of January. She believed it was the Spirit of my grandfather letting her know he was still with her and watching over the family. She would say it was a sign and the change in her was always wonderful to behold. I was thankful that my Aunt Rose and my mom kept photos of those I never got to meet; this gave me another way to be able to validate those on my maternal side of the family.

I even went to Catholic school until the 8th grade and marched in processions for Our Lady of Mt. Carmel and St. Elizabeth's Church, in my hometown of Bristol, Rhode Island and received my confirmation at the age of 14. I was always asked to march because I had an "angel gown" made by my Vo-Vo, and I truly loved playing the part of an angel here on earth as a youngster.

Whenever possible, I helped the nuns to prepare the church for services, cleaning the altar and readying the flowers for any service that may be scheduled. I really enjoyed this part of my Catholic upbringing. Yet, there always seemed to be something missing; something I could not quite explain. In fact "the calling" was so great I almost went to New Jersey to enter the convent and become a nun. My cousin Rose actually did go to the convent but came home after only 3 months. It was her experience that made me feel it was not what I was looking for.

I do give those men and women who honor their calling to the Infinite in that way, much credit for pursuing their path.

Although I attended a Catholic school and attended mass every Sunday and, of course, "holy days of obligation" (never did get the obligation part right), it seemed like I knew something else was going on around me that I could only sense and not see. It was hard to explain even then. I had to ignore what I was feeling and sensing most of the time. Yet, I knew I was different and because of my very Catholic background I was afraid to talk about it, especially in a Catholic school. As far as the "obligation days" went; it seemed to me you should not be obliged to go anywhere to talk to God on certain days. You should be able to pray freely, when you choose, and not have to pay for it.

My parents, Margaret (Perry) Mazza and Pasquale Mazza were strict Catholics. Yet they were very open minded and believed in acceptance of all religions and encouraged me to investigate other religions. They encouraged me to investigate other religions, so I did!

My mom's best friend was Jewish when she was a young girl working at one of the factories in Bristol on a "victory shift" during World War II, a time when it was not "in" to be friends with anyone German or from the Jewish faith. My mom and her family felt quite differently. Friendship should not be based on one's religious persuasion. Although their lives have taken on different priorities, they still communicate and that friendship still continues to this day. Spirit has been good to them, they are both in their 90's and still in communication.

This is part of the diversity I grew up with in the 1950s and 1960s. I feel this understanding of all religious beliefs started with my ancestors, I just keep expanding the path in a different way. Yet, I still felt there was something missing.

Because of my mother's friendship with her Jewish friend, Shirley, it opened the doors for me to pursue my interest in different religions and my friendship with those of the different religious beliefs in the years that followed The generations stayed friends. Nancy, Shirley's daughter, and I spent many summers together and we were close for most of my adolescence. This enabled me to get a bird's-eye view of Judaism. In the summer we would take turns staying at each other's houses. She would stay at my house in Bristol and I would stay at her house in Warwick. She learned about Christianity, and I about her Jewish religion and customs. Nancy always said she was going to marry a Portuguese boy…. and she did!

We also had friends that were Episcopalian or Protestant. Although very Catholic, by the amount of Catholic churches we had in Bristol at that time, our small community was pretty diversified as far as religion goes. I was interested in what was going on in all the churches. I needed to decide for myself what the diversity was all about. As a young girl I just could not see why certain people could not associate with certain other people because of their religion or color of their skin for that matter. My parents did not think that way so to me it was still all the same Infinite God. Fortunately I still feel that way! I felt very lucky to grow up learning a little about many religious beliefs.

Later on in my metaphysical studies of Hinduism, Buddhism and Muslim religions, diversity was only lightly touched upon. I have found that at the root of all these beliefs, including Catholicism, there remains two major tenants: belief in the afterlife and that there is one all-knowing Being!

Diversity comes in many ways. At a young age I learned acceptance of homosexuality through close friends, Smitty and Laura, they were like family. In my young years they were like an added aunt and uncle, and in later year's very good friends. Laura had a cousin that was "gay". At first I thought it was because he was happy all the time, because he was. As I grew in body and mind I learn that it was a label for men who were attracted to men, but it was already instilled in me to accept them and not allow judgment on that reason alone. I have met many of those who are attracted to the same sex; they are smart, understanding and courageous. In the 50s and 60s it was not understood at all! This early acceptance actually helped me in years to come, in acceptance of all sexual persuasions and religious pursuits. This does not change the person they are inside. My family was so accepting of all people and their religious beliefs, I believe this helped me in the work I do now. Unknowingly all my experience and understanding of diversity as a young girl and later into womanhood prepared me for my future in a very gentle way.

# Chapter 2
# My Later Years

As I grew older, I married, divorced, married again and divorced again. During that time I stopped any investigation of religion I had started in my early life. But…I still had these nagging thoughts and ideas in the back of my mind that I could not speak about. There was very little talk of "psychic" or "medium", in the late 50s and 60s and even 70s, in my little world of family and friends. I was not a flower child, nor did I go to college to meet those very different from myself. I was just a normal person getting married for the first time at 18, having a miscarriage and divorced at 19. Later I realized that this was part of my path. In my younger years I was too upset and concerned about myself to realize then that I had to go through what I did to become the person I am today.

The miscarriage and two divorces gave me the insight of what pain was like and the stigma attached to divorced women at that time. Some women going through an unwanted divorce still go through that pain and social stigma. Society always seems more understanding for the men that are alone, but they are still having a hard time with women taking a stand for themselves. I am here today to try to help you leave the past in the past and improve your future even if you do not want to communicate with the so-called "dead".

The pain and confusion any of you are going through, I have also experienced. I also did not let it get the better of me. I made a choice to find out what the Universe and the God above intended. You see, in bringing to the mothers I communicate for, infants from the side of Spirit that never made it to this life; I do understand their pain.

I met and married my second husband, Ed at the age of 20. We had 15 good years together (13 of them married) but the 15<sup>th</sup> year wasn't that great. We were both very family oriented and spent most of our Saturday evening's playing cards with family and friends. One of Ed's aunts, Jan, read playing cards, mostly for family entertainment, and she was pretty good at it. She taught me a little of her skill and this was my first introduction in using a tool to foretell the future. I also started dabbling in the crystal ball at that time. I had to keep it a secret though, since Ed did not approve. It was soon after this, in the 13th year of our marriage, when we divorced under friendly terms. Sorry, no grimy mess in courts here, I can't help it, I am an Aquarius, we like things as peaceful as possible. I kept in touch with him for a while and I still send holiday cards to his family. They have always meant quite a lot to me. You see, they were part of my life, my learning and growth.

I say that because looking back on my life, I learned something from everyone I have come in contact with. I have realized that I also gave something to them. This something I talk about is spiritual growth. It is there for all of us if we choose to take our experiences, good or bad and turn them into learning experiences.

My mother always told me that if you were thirsty and the glass was not full you could look at it in two ways- negative: the glass is ½ empty or the positive: the glass is ½ full. I chose the ½ full glass.

Shortly after parting from Ed, I met my friend Christine. We were going through the same life style changes, "divorce". We partied, met new friends, and traveled a lot together. Later as we began to settle down we went our separate ways, Chris, furthering her education in the business world and I, in the Spirit world. Our separation was only because of the choices we had made about our paths in life. I am grateful for her in my life, as we both needed each other at the time. She is doing well and I do miss her.

I met Carolyn through friends at the beauty shop I worked in, Trendsetters in Bristol. My life had been a little boring. No traveling, or meeting new people, but I was pretty happy. I was starting to get very involved in Spirit Communication for myself. This was the time I met people with the same interests as I had. I could only call them acquaintances because I really only saw them at class or for coffee afterwards. It was a time that I was learning to ask my deceased relatives, friends and my Spirit guides for help in getting what I felt I needed in my life.

Although I had taken my parents and my aunts, Rose, Irene and their friend Beatie on many trips, I felt I did need a traveling companion, closer to my own age. It was by coincidence that Carolyn was having her hair done and we got into a conversation about Disney. I mentioned that Disney World is one of my most favorite places on this earth. Next thing you know we were there. Thank you Carolyn! We made about five trips to the Grand Floridian at Disney World and a few to other places, including Boston for first nights. I learned about food and traveling, and enjoyed her family as she enjoyed mine. I learned so much from Carolyn and Ida, that on a personal nature the details are too numerous to mention. I thank them for the joy and understanding they brought into my life. They also helped me to improve my quality of life and to look at different types of lifestyles. They both have a hand in rounding out my education in a more formal, realistic way.

During these ten years I did date a little but I found no one with the same interests as I had or anyone I was attracted to. So my family and those that accepted my beliefs were my world. I became more and more involved in the Metaphysical realms, learning about meditation, chakras, tarot, scrying, herbal remedies, and understanding of Goddess ritual and spirit communication. My teachers were many and it was a time that was MYSTERIOUS, FANTASTIC AND WONDEROUS!

# Chapter 3
## Guidance and My Pathway to Spirit

Many people stop and ask themselves "why am I here"? I decided to make it a point that my interests would tell me "why I was here", and if I never really found the answer to that question, it was okay, I would enjoyed the ride. White Light Books in Cranston, Rhode Island was one of a very few metaphysical store that I was aware of at the time. I am sure there were more stores of that type, but my teachers would come from White Light Books for quite some time. Also, at that time 22 years ago I had NO idea where the mystery would take me, but while I searching, I would enjoy every minute!

Diverse as the teachers were, they were what I was looking for to unravel the mystery of things. At the age of 37 I started to have dreams that were actually happening on the earth plane. Jeannette, a medium teaching awareness of Spirit in the early 1990s was the first person that encouraged my abilities to communicate with those in spirit. She also helped me to understand my dreams, an important aspect for those who are just beginning and want communication of some kind with a loved one on the "side of Spirit".

After 2-3 years of study of "the unseen" I found myself reading Tarot at White Light Books. This also started by "accident". One day while I was at the store the owner, Gloria, needed someone to do a reading and asked if I would. Of course, I did not think I was good enough but did I learn something that day, to trust that "Spirit" knows when you are ready. At that time I used Tarot cards and a crystal ball and it was great. I actually thought I was helping people, and earning a few extra dollars doing it. I had already known that "Spirit" was there but I still thought I needed a tool to contact the forces of light in the universe. In reality, it took me a while to realize most of the information I was giving to people was directly from "Spirit", the guides and loved ones of those I was reading for as well as my own. I dove into meditating more and more to learn about my guides and in doing so I learned more about myself.

I worked on and off at Gloria's for about a year but then "Spirit" had something else in mind for me; a full time job with health benefits. After graduating from my business courses, I began working at a drug and alcohol rehab center in the office. I worked there for five years before leaving and acquiring a position closer to home at a psychologist's office, where I worked for four years and then left to communicate with "Spirit" on a full time basis. From these positions and the people in them, I learned more about from a psychological point of view. This helped me to know when any of my clients might need to seek professional help for bereavement. Oh yes, the God/Goddess above and my Spirit Guides knew what they were doing. Although I still kept up with my interests, I had to stop my visits to White Light Books when I acquired a full-time position.

Now, I do not expect everyone out there to do as I did. It was a lot easier for me to meditate and communicate with spirit on a very regular basis because I had been and still was living back home with mom and dad. I had no children or husband to take care of. I helped with the outside chores and painting the house and mom and dad took care of me. Mom was back in her element and dad had someone besides mom to communicate with. Mom and dad enjoyed me back home as much as I enjoyed being taken care of.

After a while I knew that I did not need tools like the tarot or crystal ball. I had a direct line to the Universe and Spirit. Someone described it once as "the 800 number to the Infinite". It was around that time 1989, I think, that I was introduced to my first experience at a Spiritualist church. Jean, my first teacher, took me to the Plymouth Spiritualist Church, in Plymouth, Massachusetts. I remember it well; Jeannette took five of her students camping to Miles Standish State Park, (great place) and decided to introduce us to a Spiritualist church service.

I still remember the medium that prophesized through my maternal grandmother, Vo-Vo, that I would be doing exactly what she (the medium) was doing up at the podium in front of people at a church service. Although I felt my grandmother was with me, my internal self-denial said, "Yeah, right!" Me, the person who would get physically sick when reading a book report in front of the class when I was in school, there was no way I was going to get up in front of people. This same person, me, is afraid to make changes when ordering from a menu because the waitress may get upset. I am going to stand in front of a room full of people and give them messages from someone they could not see and prove the continuity of life, too! Boy, was I in for the ride of my life!

It was then that my <u>parents</u> found the first Spiritualist Church of Onset, in Onset, Massachusetts located on the west side of the Cape Cod Canal. Services are on Sunday evenings at 6:30 p.m. and are very convenient for me to attend with my parents and aunts. This was my first formal introduction to lessons from a Spiritualist. Reverend Kenneth Custance was the Pastor of the Onset Spiritualist Church for about 70 years.

Rev. Kenneth was about as old as Abraham in the bible; he still had his wits about him and was a very good teacher and medium. I attended classes with Rev. Kenneth on and off for about a year and a half then I was led to a church closer to my home. Rev. Custance is now in Spirit form and is still teaching and guiding those here on the earth plane that wish to learn from him. My husband and I now serve his church as speaker and medium on a regular basis.

One of my teachers from White Light Books was a woman called "Eclipse". She was a Goddess Priestess and Native American drummer and we became steadfast friends for a few years. We have the same birth date, February 13, 1950. She led me to my path of understanding myself as a woman and healer. I learned through "goddess ritual" how to go deep inside of myself and heal the past. Using her drum, she would take us on a journey deep into the earth. At times I actually could feel the heart beat of the earth itself. It was there I found my true self. It was there I started to understand what I was capable of. I was starting to see my own future through journeying, or guided meditation. It was wonderful, and we all accepted each other for our strengths and helped each other build upon that. Those years were absolutely wonderful and "Spirit" knew what they were doing when they sent me back to school at the age of 40 to learn new business skills. I would not be typing this now if they did not. Then by the age of 45 I finally knew who I was and what I wanted. But…leaving it up to the "powers that be", I was still in for more surprises.

The journeying and meditation helped me to lose my inhibitions caused by the hurts of the past and turn those hurts into lessons I could look at in a positive light. My years with Native American women's circles and goddess ritual helped me understand myself as well as other women I was to meet in my future. This time was a continuation in learning about diversity in religion, relationships and genders.

My path was already laid out for me. My community and those I worked and lived with would be my higher education. I did not realize it then, but as a hair stylist for 30 years I learned a lot about people and how to keep something in confidence. This is very important in the work I do now, working for "Spirit" in a public arena. Psychology and understanding of people is a life-long, never ending lesson.

I was communicating with my maternal grandmother. I was very close to her and my mother's sisters, Irene and Rose all of their lives, and mine until they passed to Spirit. They were my babysitters when my brother and I were young. I took care of my aunts for about a year and a half before I could not any longer. I was the daughter they never had. Both my aunts have passed and communicate with me regularly. I have even received comfort from one of them via electronic voice phenomena also known as "EVP".

My grandmother, Lucy, was my first guide. She had been in Spirit for about 15 years when I started on my path with Spirit. She gave me information about my mother's family that I never knew. She told me stories about my mom and her sisters and the things they used to get into when they were young, and also about people I had never met from mom's side of the family - this was later confirmed by my mother and aunts.

During the time I dabbled a little in Goddess and Pagan religions, I was getting a lot of confirmed information from Spirit. Yes, I was still searching for something that encompassed what I believe in, that there is an existence of some sort after our body ceases to exist on this earth plane.

I was meditating on a steady basis since going back to get more education. The meditating kept me at peace with myself and helped me realize my own potential. Yes, I am still human and I still have a tough time realizing that God gave human beings "FREE WILL", and even the ability to communicate with the unseen. This book is not only a mini-history of my spiritual and physical path on this earth plane, but a lesson for everyone who reads it, and makes a choice; to add to your own potential of spirit communication or sit on the sidelines. If you ask your Spirit loved ones for help they will be there for you. Pay attention to the little messages they send to you daily and in your dreams. Use your own internal "awareness"!

Once I was introduced to the community of Spiritualism and Spiritualist churches my eyes were really opened. I stopped using tools entirety and started to use what I thought was my imagination. It was not my imagination; it was what Spirit people were sending me. It is my belief that anyone having the true desire to receive communication from his or her dearly departed may do so in one way or another.

# Chapter 4
## My Driving Force

My parents were my driving force in my younger years. I feel I had the best parents in the world. My Dad, now in spirit, guides me and helps me and others in areas he is proficient in. Mom is 92+ years old as this book is being written yet still has a special force of her own. She is very active; bowling twice a week, playing cards and attending aerobics classes.

My early teachers helped me build trust with my guides and loved ones on the side of spirit. I always wrote down the information I received and I still have those writings. I am finding that much of the information is still in the process of happening. One of the "messages" given to me by spirit was that I should not decline an invitation for coffee. Boy I did not understand that one at all at the time. My grandmother knew what she was talking about because about six months after that message and more of them regarding my future, I met my husband, Brian. And. believe it or not, I met him in a meditation group at a Spiritualist church and accepted his invitation for coffee after services!

I write about my family and myself because I want you all to know that I am not a super human being that can connect with the Spirit side at any time. I had to learn to put up barriers and inform my guides that I am in charge, not them. No, I am only a human being just like you and my family is just like yours. I worked as a hairdresser for over 30 years and then worked as a secretary/receptionist at a drug and alcohol rehab center. Then I worked at a psychotherapist's office closer to home. I felt Spirit had put me in these positions to learn to deal with people. I do not have a formal higher education. The knowledge I did need Spirit has given me through my pathway in life.

Today and since the day we met, my husband is the catalyst. He believed in me, just as my parents had believed in me when I was younger.

Brian was the one who asked me for a cup of coffee (as my grandmother had said) after a Spiritualist service at the First Spiritualist Church of Brockton, then located in Somerset, Massachusetts. I had become a regular at the services and we both attended Psychomertry and Spirit communication classes regularly. This is where we became friends. There are many things that happened during our romance (like him bringing me flowers on our first date and, of course, the coffee thing), which Spirit had predicted. I grew to love very deeply this gentle, kind, and loving man, who believed in the existence of "Spirit", yet consistently had to find physical ways to prove it. Our courtship was like a fairytale; he was so romantic, like reading a romance novel. But that is not what I am here to talk about. It is about our both finding a home with Spirit. In believing that those that have passed on can help you and can communicate with you; we have made this our way of life.

There are many things that happened in our personal and spiritual life when we both knew that loved ones and guides had worked hard to put us both on the paths that led us up to our future together.
Brian's sister is a medium, and he had been introduced to Spiritualism about 30 years before I had. His life, like mine, had taken him down a path with a family of his own, until now.

We went to Spiritualist churches together, sometimes three services in one day. It was fun and exciting to watch different mediums work. I knew what I wanted to aspire to, and what I did not want to do.

Our first trip together was in 1997 to San Francisco, California; we visited a haunted restaurant in Chinatown and Spiritualist churches. We both had readings regarding our life together with Spirit yet it was still hard to believe. Little did we know we would be working with churches in New England and across the country in the years to come. We just enjoyed each other's company and the best part is we enjoyed everything the other enjoyed too. We both liked dining out, Sci-Fi movies, books and spirit. What more could a girl ask for?

Brian convinced me that I was good enough to start giving "Spirit greetings" at church services after I gave him a message about his dog, Daisy. The pastor in charge allowed me to give one or two messages at the time, and that was enough for me. Well here was another Spirit prediction coming true! I just let Spirit guide me and I kept going from then on.

On our second trip in 1999 we decided to go to Las Vegas, Nevada, and Sedona, Arizona. Yeah! Although we are not gamblers, there are many shows to see in Vegas so off we went. First we went to Sedona where Brian had a whole bunch of surprises waiting for me. One of which was a beautiful helicopter ride to one of Sedona's plateaus. There was a gourmet dinner waiting for us. As we said good-by to the helicopter I remember thinking," I hope he remembers where he left us". After all, it was a long way down and it looked like we were the only ones on earth. For two hours we were the only ones on this high mesa, surrounded by the beautiful desert mountains and expansive vistas of Sedona, Arizona. Little did I know Brian was going to ask me to become his bride. (I did bring a white suit just in case) after all what happens in Las Vegas does not always stay in Las Vegas. A few days later we were married at the "Little Chapel of the Flowers" in Las Vegas on April 15, 1999 with my nephew Joel in attendance.

Spirit worked in mysterious ways for more reasons than I can count. After working two jobs for five years, Brian asked me to leave CODAC and the beauty shop for something closer to home. It also happened at that time my Aunts Rose and Irene, who lived together and needed more care. So, I stopped my working positions and cared for my lovely aunts, who in my younger years cared for my brother and I while my mom and dad worked. They fared better as we had fun for the last year they would be together on this earth plane. This too, taught me much about a loved one's passing. My Brian was heaven sent; our relatives on the "Side of Spirit" knew what they were doing.

Aunt Rose passed in 1999 and shortly thereafter Irene had a stroke and had to be placed in a nursing home where I was able to see her on a daily basis. If Brian was not in my life, these lovely ladies would not had the attention I was able to give them, the same attention they gave me when I was young. Later I will tell you of the messages I received from my relatives since they have passed.

# Chapter 5
## Living the Truth-Working Together

Brian had been taking the Morris Pratt Course in Spiritualism and he convinced me to do so also. It is through this correspondence course, classes taken at the Spiritualist church and the knowledge that I gained in the past that led me to become a certified medium, Brian to become a commissioned healer, and our ordination as ministers of Spiritualism.

In the fall of 2003 Brian convinced me to open a small office near our home. We have a very good landlord, Ben who was open to what we did even though he did not believe in "such things". He has the belief of "live and let live" as well as "to each their own".

Brian and I work together for Spiritualist churches and at our Kent Spiritual Center, in Warren, Rhode Island, to further our knowledge of Spirit in whatever way we can. In doing so, we try to bring classroom lessons to the public, the people who desire spiritual information and to learn about the unseen and do not know where to find it. We bring information to the public that will be of interest to them as well as to help them in their quest to communicate with loved ones and to raise their vibration on this earth plane.

As I began to be more popular with the general public, we needed more room. When I had two rooms, Spirit told me I would be doing more communicating for them and will need three rooms. Even though I trusted my guides, I told them I liked it where I was and wanted to stay. Our center was on a main road, convenient, quiet and at the time two minutes from my home. In 2005 the office I moved into became available, and in the same building! Spirit was correct again! This new office does have three rooms, is reasonably priced and is just what Spirit described. This office space has worked out well for us and we have developed classes for all who seek truth. The classes we have developed are for: obtaining your personal EVP (electronic voice phenomena), remote viewing, dreams, symbolism, animal symbols, chakra and Solfeggio tuning, aura, meaning of colors in meditation, angel 101, table tipping, the power of positive thinking and trance, transformation, transfiguration and one of most "think outside of the box" class on secrets of orb photography. We are constantly looking for ways to help "prove the continuity of life". In my own reality, Spirit said: "Build it and they will come". They did! I do very little advertising; Spirit sends those in need to me, as they said they would.

In January of 2007 Brian and I were made Co-Directors of the Department of Phenomenal Evidence for the National Spiritual Association of Churches. Investigating spirit phenomena and doing a monthly article for the National Spiritualist Summit magazine has been quite rewarding, and we are both still learning and growing together with help from Spirit.

In the following chapter you will read about some of those I have read for. They are only a sampling of what I feel Spirit has had in mind for me when I embarked on this path many years ago. As well as serving Spiritualist churches together, I do many "reading parties" at the homes of my clients. This has brought people in need to me that otherwise would not have been able to find the solace they needed in their bereavement.

I am still a normal working class woman with grandchildren and grandnephews I love dearly. With all Spirit has given me in my years working with them, they keep on giving.

Although I do not utilize the writing journals now, I do still have them. I find that, even now, much of the information I wrote in complete faith years ago is still unfolding in my life with Brian.

# Part Two
# Continuity of Life

The philosophy of Spiritualism is based on two concepts about life after death.

1. Spirits are real people, human beings: men, woman and children stripped of their outer garment of flesh, which still possess a real, substantial body that we know as the spiritual body.

2. The Spirit World is a real world, just as real to Spirits functioning though their Spirit bodies as the physical world is to us.

Basically what occurs at death (of the body) is the departure from one state of consciousness to a different one. When we transition, we keep our same memories, habits, ideas, and the need to care for those we left behind. The person in spirit is allowed to grow if he or she chooses to change. In the next few chapters you will gain a greater understanding of this concept.

To prove that one still exists after so-called death, we do not need haunting or ghostly apparitions because Spirit loved ones to communicate in many ways. Some of the techniques used on a regular basis are clairvoyance of all types (subjective or objective), table tipping, and electronic voice communication commonly known as EVP. It is always more difficult to use any of these techniques to "prove" who is communicating, but it can be done (more on this and other types of communication with Spirit, later).

As a certified medium with the National Spiritualist Association of Churches, headquartered in Lily Dale, New York, I must "prove continuity of life" to those I communicate for. I take this very seriously and feel the responsibility Spirit has placed me with is important in every way possible.

Proof of the continuity of life can be established in Spirit messages by the medium giving names, description of the person in Spirit, habits, memories, way of passing, important dates, the way spirit had of saying a certain thing, identifying a specific piece of jewelry, and/or knowledge of experiences with the person from the Spirit side of life and many more. The following chapters are my proof given to and accepted by those I have read.

# Chapter 6
## Sari & Baby

LYNN: Sari called me about 9 p.m. on a Sunday night sounding devastated and in tears. She had found me in the Yellow Pages and was drawn to my ad "Afterlife Readings". I was in the middle of getting ready to relax and retire for the evening and almost did not answer the phone. It may have been just laziness on my part after a very busy Sunday of readings and classes, but my guides thought differently, so I answered the phone. Something in her voice sounded desperate. Instantly I knew she was not a crackpot when her opening sentence was "You may think I am a little flakey but".… I knew instantly that I could not put her off even at this late hour. She explained to me that she was desperate to find her little kitty that was like a soul mate to her. Her kitty, "Baby", had not been home for three days and this was not like Simba, and at times also called him Baby. We made an appointment for the following Wednesday, and as Spirit always makes sure I am in the right place at the right time, I ended up seeing Sari a day earlier. Because of Sari's inability to leave the house and my desire to get a sense of the area that Simba was familiar with, I went to Sari's home.

Yes people, Sari's kitty had not returned. If you are one of those thousands that have felt the closeness of a cherished pet from the other side of life, you know that they are still with you, loving you and protecting you. It is not unusual for an animal to enter the reading especially if the client wants to hear from their pet. Animals are honest and loving. They will always "be there" for us, whether it be here or from the other side of life. When you lose a parent, child or an animal, we all have to deal with the loss in our own way. Some of us need help.

Sari: "Lynn you were starting to pick up Simba like crazy for a few days before. He had disappeared on Thursday and by Saturday I was going "machugana" (Sari's word for crazy). The reason I feel my story

27

belongs in your book is because my whole view of finding you in the first place was a feeling of powerlessness. I knew that day when he was 2 hours late; I was never going to see him again. My greatest concern was that he was injured and hurt and suffering somewhere. Remember, those days were raining and horrible and cold. I was devastated to think that his little body was being ravaged by nature and the elements. I found you in the phone book and on a Sunday night I thought for sure I was going to get an answering machine and instead I got you. You were so kind and so real to me that there was a connection of trust. You told me that you felt that I was correct in my feelings but it may be too soon because of the closeness of his passing. You were going to come to me on a Wednesday because you were going to be in Warwick but you ended up coming on Tuesday".

"When you first started, you described my uncle that I was not too close to, and I could not figure out why Baby would be with him and not with someone I was close to. You said that this uncle was helping Simba to get to where he needs to go. This all happened in my living room at that time I had Baby's favorite chair there and you sat in it and started giving me all kinds of information that you could in no way have known. I just knew that Simba was communicating through you in some way".

"We went into Jacob's (Sari's son) bedroom and you were immediately attracted to Baby's blanket and you put your left palm down on the blanket. You told me about charkas opening up wide and the energy coming from that blanket. You also gave me more confirmation about Baby. That was Baby's blanket"! (Sari called Simba, Baby)

"You had told me during the reading that Simba was safe and very happy. He was getting as much shrimp and lobster, as he wanted. It was his way of letting me know it was truly him, he loved shrimp and lobster and we fed it to him all the time, and that he was truly happy and he was being treated really well. During the reading you kept asking if he had a red collar on him. You kept seeing a red collar. You had told me that a car had hit him but someone had honored his little

28

body and put him to rest. Because you kept seeing this red around the neck my thoughts were that he had broken his neck or something. You also described a cat he was following and you saw that other cat walk across a dangerous street and he tried to follow. I had told you then that I knew of the cat you were talking about. Two hours after you left that day, I was looking out my front window and I saw that cat I was thinking of…that cat was wearing the red collar. I think you were picking that up because it may have been the last thing Baby saw".

"You then turned your attention to Spike, (Baby's best friend-cat in our home) and you laid your hand on him. Although he sort of bolted when you first came into Jake's bedroom he did not move when you approached him and the minute you laid your hand on Spike I noticed that Spike was purring and purring and purring, like you were giving comfort to him too. You mentally started to introduce yourself to Spike and told him who you were and what you were doing. I could see him opening up to you. In fact it is hard to hear you and I speaking in some areas of the (taped) reading at that time because all you can hear is Spike licking the microphone. Spike had communicated to you, "Why did they take him away from me"? You made him understand that Simba (Baby) was not taken away; he went out for a walk and was with the Angels. Although he still looks for "Baby", Spike is much better since that day. He was like the dominant mother/father cat to Simba. He always protected him and loved him dearly".

"You started to describe the front door and Baby coming back. (Personality wise or a reincarnation) You explained that there would be another kitty that was in need of a family. You also said that I might find two. We did search shelters soon after your visit because although no animal would take the place of Simba, Jake and I were going downhill fast. I felt the sooner we had another animal to divert our attention the better, especially my son. We knew we could not replace him, but we needed something. You said we would just know by looking at the animal that it was the right one. I thought at first I pushed it a little too soon in my grief, however, with both their unique personalities, we ended up with two "Izzie" and "Simon" became healers in our life. Simba's personality was so unique that we needed both of these lost babies to help us heal. My son, Jake has bonded so well with Izzie and Simon. Together they sort of make up for Simba's personality. We love them both and Spike is getting on with both of them but he never stops looking for Simba. He has taken to looking out the window since Baby has gone, I do not know maybe he sees something that we cannot. You also told me about some of the subtle things to look for as far as Spirit was concerned and there are times now when I sit in Baby's chair at a particular window that I sometimes feel a soft stroke across my cheek or my hair move. You also told me to be aware of what took place at bedtime between the stages of just being awake and just getting into sleep. I found that when playing a certain sound on the sleep machine, at that point when wakefulness meets sleep, I hear Baby as I do on the EVP of our first part of the first tape I did with you. As far as my Baby is concerned you have brought me much peace".

LYNN:  During Sari's reading for Simba, (Baby) her parents and other relatives came into the reading and that is where the healing really began.

Sari: "Lynn, you described my dad to me and I had asked you some questions, like is it pop or soda and you said something about a river and I said St. Croix then you said river again. You were like a kid at Christmas, you got so excited, you said wow, what is that, started laughing and then you said: "is that a dog at the bow of the boat"? There was no way you could have known that my dad always went out with his dog on the river, all the time, it made so much sense to me. I said, "That's my dad". Then I gave you a woman's name and the physical changes that came over you and the emotion that bowled you over with her, your body language sort of closed in and you were observing what was going on within yourself, I knew it was my mother. You said she needed to be invited, and I could see many reasons why my mother would have to be invited to speak to me. You see, I talk to my dad all the time but I have never talked to my mother. You said you were getting such a rush of love that you seldom felt that it was hard to explain. My mom at that time, through you, started to apologize for so much. She told you there was so much that she had missed out on, so much where I was concerned and needed forgiveness. I asked you to tell her that I understood completely about her illness and there was no need to apologize but it gave me an immense amount of peace".

"You also brought through my grandmother, you kept saying something about the earrings, and the true confirming thing about that was that my grandmother got me my very first pair of good earrings. I had not thought of that in over 30 years and I had to even ask my sister about that. I asked her if she remembered if our grandmother came with us to buy the earrings and what they looked like and she said gold-filled cameos, which you described to a "T". You also said "studs" but my grandma corrected you and said "posts" because she said that "studs" was an inappropriate word to use. You then asked me if this was a "particularly religious woman" and I just cracked up because my grandmother was very Jewish, very kosher, very religious and very proper. She also had many ideas about my family that I didn't agree with.

"It is incredible the healing that has taken place, because of the people that came through you, my mother, father and my grandmother and the messages they had for me. I am still astounded that it was Baby that led me to this other incredible healing".

"Lynn you also conveyed to me the understanding that they were happier, they are getting along and were still trying to help those that were left here on this plane. You kept saying "unconditional love". You did not know or could not know the hell my father's family was. These people were walking dysfunction definitions. You, through Simba, and through my need to seek my little kitten's beautiful Spirit, provided me with peace and opened the door for me to understand and work on forgiving with these people. They, through a ripple effect, really messed up when they were alive".

"I tried to talk to my father's brother, who is still alive, about some of the things you said to me. He was not hearing It though, he will not accept the "life after death thing". Yet when I asked him about the numbers you kept giving me, like an address 222 or 22—. I asked my uncle what the address was where he grew. He said don't you remember? Uncle Shoi lived only a few blocks up the road from where you lived on _____St. you were 2100 they were 222...something. To me that was my uncle Shoji's way of saying that they were so close but yet so far apart. My dad and his brother did not speak. My living uncle never asked how you knew that, Lynn but I think he is still wondering".

"What I got from my session with you was an overwhelming sense of well being, peace and a weight lifted. Many questions were put to rest. When people pass from this life, I have always had the trust that they are going to a better place even though we all have our own perceptions about that. You confirmed to me that they do and try to be better people once there. Thank you".

LYNN: Sari had many personal closures that day I went to visit her for confirmation that her "Baby" was in heaven. Yet, because of her love for this gentle animal she received peace of another sort with many of her relatives on the side of Spirit. There is much more confirmation that Sari had given to me about what I had told her. I have left them out of this book because those messages were for herself and her family.

# Chapter 7
# Colleen

Colleen is a young married woman from Newport, Rhode Island, with very good friends that have had me for "reading parties" at their home. I do this quite often and have learned much from it. Many have parties yearly. Colleen has been at two parties and here is what she had to say.

Colleen: "I have had 2 readings with You and at first my mother was still alive in February 2004, I was a little disappointed initially because I thought for sure my grandmother was going to come through. It happened that people I really did not know came through and I was not sure at the time who they were. I guess I just truly wanted to hear from my grandmother because I was close to her, I just took it for granted it would be her that would give me the message. You gave me very specific details about who was there. Having the tape was very helpful as when I listened to it again and I discovered more information than what I actually listened to that night. One of the specific things was that you described a woman holding a baby and she asked if I knew who had lost an unborn child or very young child because this grandmotherly woman was caring for the tiny soul. In fact I had had 2 miscarriages one of them actually pretty far along and with the information on the tape we, my husband and I, discovered that it was my husband's grandmother caring for our unborn child. Now the interesting thing is that when we listened to his tape with the reading that my husband had with you back in November, 2003 we realize that the same person by description was in his reading holding the baby and it was his grandmother".

At this point a question was asked if Colleen thought that Lynn might have put 2 and 2 together. Colleen's answer was; "No she did not know that my husband was my husband at the time. My reading was in February 2004 and his was in November 2003. Linda J. Kent

There was another gentleman that came through in the reading, specifics were given, and he kept giving me vegetables, you said that he made her feel that the "giving" part was very significant to him, she specifically said not a farm but a small garden. He was also wearing suspenders and glasses. I could not identify him then but my mom and dad could. I believe it was my great grandfather; he lived in the city but had a small patch of land behind the house where he use to grow tomatoes and peppers then give them out to people in the neighborhood, and he indeed wore glasses and suspenders.

"The other woman who came in was very different indeed she wore her hair in a bun and had an old fashion dress on and she was standing by me in the reading and showing you how cute I was as a child, she rubbing my face and the significant thing about this person that I could identify with was her shoes, they were very black and the soles were very thick. When I spoke to my mom she remembered that her grandmother had shoes like that. Mom said when my great-grandmother was a little girl she broke her leg and could only wear black shoes and one had to have a very thick sole so she could walk more normally because of the damage done to the leg when she was a child. Of course I did not know any of this but upon finding out "information from mom" I thought this was a good form of identification and it was something that you could not have even begun to guess at".

"You then asked me if I knew anyone in the family who died of "alcoholism" and if I wanted to speak to him. (I always ask about alcoholics because they might not have had positive energy when they were here and the client may not want to communicate with them if they are not "healed" on the side of Spirit.) At the time of the reading I kind of said "no", and he went away. Later I remembered I had an uncle that was indeed an alcoholic, a homeless person and he chose not to keep in touch with the family. He indeed had passed of complications due to alcoholism".

"Also throughout the readings that day, it was a party at my friend Lynn's house, an older man with a turquoise station wagon was coming in to say "hello" to everyone. No one recognized him... but when you brought him to me I immediately recognized him as my grandfather. I even made sure of the station wagon with my mom it was him, I am sure. I thought the connections that were made in that reading were very interesting and with at least 1 specific identifying item from each person and the messages were very uplifting as well".

"First, before I tell you about my reading in November, I must explain to you that my mother was not too keen on me doing this. She would say things like "you know you should not be doing this or make sure you say extra prayers". I got to my friend Linda's house early because I wanted to socialize with Linda and her mom before it was my turn and there were already a few people there. You came in with your husband and set up, Brian socialized a while before he left. You usually request some "quite time" before you start your readings then come in to say you are ready and will jokingly ask who your first victim is. I was going to be the 3$^{rd}$ or 4$^{th}$ person she would be seeing that day but you came down and said: "Who knows the lady with the first name beginning with the letter "C" possibly a Carol, older, mid fifties, very anxious to speak to someone and is relatively new there, but strong". "My mom's name is Carol", I knew it had to be her. "You called me upstairs. In the reading you said (you did not know it was my mom yet) this person knew that you believed in communication with the dead, even though she did not, she realized that you believe and since she passed she has been waiting to talk to you". In that reading my mom, through you said a lot of things that made me realized it was truly she, the worries she had about my dad and brother were specific to them. She stated some of the issues and that she (mom) was still concerned with, some of which I was aware of, some I became aware of soon after my reading. My mom got pretty definite with whom she was with on the Spirit and I believed she is much more peaceful now since my communication with her, I know I am".

"You also gave me validation of certain situations that occurred when my mom was still alive. There was no way you could have known anything about these things unless mom told her. I originally had the reading because it was something I had believed in yet never through I could validate. The 2$^{nd}$ reading was much more meaningful to me especially that my mom was waiting to speak to me. The other interesting thing is that when you were talking, you took on the mannerisms of my mother. I also asked you if my aunt was there, my aunt and my mom were very close but here was a little jealously, you said your mom says, "Oh she is here somewhere". That is exactly the way my mom would say it when she was here. The other thing again was that you brought up something about my dad that you could not have known. By giving me information from my mother in the exact manner she wanted to express it, she said; "your mom is saying that this is the right person for your father and he needs someone to care for him, he is like a little boy who could not take care of himself". They had been together since they were kids. My dad went through a depression a few years ago and mom was afraid he would go the same way. She also mentioned that I should speak to my brother in order to help him understand. I know he was having trouble with the passing of my mother and with my dad having a friend, but I did understand my mom's reasoning behind this. Since that reading we have been working on this situation as a family, I think it is working out okay. This gave me peace for the fact that mom did not have to worry about dad anymore and would be there for him when his time came".

"You must understand that mom was very jealous of dad and would always needle him when he spoke to someone she did not know. I always thought these traits carried over to the other world. Hence, I believe that is one of the reasons we were not so keen on dad's new relationship. But I also believe mom always had dad's best welfare in mind. I have always read things about the afterlife and angels as well as having my own experience with these spiritual beings".

"I am much more at peace with my mom passing now, she suffered quite a bit toward the end of her life and I am looking at my dad's relationship in a different way. I also think my brother is working on this also. My dad is more like a dad now and that is the way mom wanted it".

LYNN: Traits we have here on this earth plane definitely travel with us upon leaving the physical body and moving on. You must understand that Spiritualism as a religion has certain Principles that Spiritualist's try to live by. This also carries over to the world of Spirit. Spiritualism does not have dogma or creed but we live by principles. Principle #8 states: We affirm that the doorway to reformation is never closed against any soul here or hereafter.

Meaning you can always change your mind about the way you were here on the earth plane, change your ideas, choices and look at the world differently. You have the opportunity to improve yourself, if you choose. You even love on a different level, greater and more caring; I call this the Universal God-Goddess Love. Yes I do say God-Goddess as it is within balance of both the male and female idea of love in an overwhelming natural way, protection, caring, concern, knowing and understanding most of all without thought for your own feelings.

This also includes Colleen's uncle that was trying to communicate who had an addiction here on this earth plane. He would be given the choice to rise above and help those he ignored here on earth. Colleen's mom realized that her own feelings would get in the way if she did allow her husband she left behind to be left alone. There would be much more burden on Colleen and possibly her brother. Carol wants everyone to be happy, including her husband she left behind, yet she knew he needed help to move forward.

Spirit sometimes puts that help in front of us, yet we are too blind to see at times. Open your eyes and your heart if you have a loved one that was left behind by their mate. What do they need? Don't ask or think about what your needs are. This is the ultimate in Spiritual love and understanding.

# Chapter 8
## Jane

Jane: "I have always believed there was something more to death than death itself, you came very highly recommended by Colleen so I thought I would like to communicate with my Grandmother. Some of the reading was very specific which surprised me. I did not expect specifics. You related my grandmother to me in a very loving and comforting way just as my grandmother would have done if she were still here; we had a very special relationship. People came through that I did not think would come through; I guess I had tunnel vision when it came to who would want to speak to me. You held my hand and told me that someone was here that did not want me to let go and this is how this person was, it was the sort of relationship we had, it was my grandmother, you also hugged me the way my grandmother hugged me. She came out with a name and a person in uniform that I knew exactly whom it was. I was overwhelmed by how accurate you were."

"My husband's uncle came through by his name, Tom. You said he was fun, the life of the party and was doing something with carpentry. He was very close to my husband and although I did not know him, I understood that he was fun, the life of the party and always ready to help his family. He used to build his own beautiful furniture. You gave me a message specifically for my husband Andrew, that he was proud of him and to give him a pat on the back. That actually blew me away".

"Also a very close friend of my husband's who was killed in Iraq and he came through, I recognized his description in uniform and that he was fishing and he loved to fish. He was not ready when it happened and Chris, through you, said he had a friend with him when he passed. The both of them were having a hard time getting use to the fact they were not in a physical body anymore and they were still tied to this earth plane. He still had unfinished business here and wanted to get a message to his wife but she would not at this time be ready to hear that 'she must let go' He has been around her and is worried. Jane, my friend, also stated that her husband and some of the men at work recognized that this young man's Spirit had been around. You also brought my grandmother on my dad's side of the family, a wonderful surprise and she spoke about my father's health, which is something my brother and I have been concerned about.

LYNN: This young soldier pass in October 2004 and this was spring 2005 but many times those on the side of Spirit need to let their loved ones know they want them to move on because of the love they carry with them. Although he was in a war torn area, this was the type of crossing that was not expected. When this happens it is like putting your Spirit body into a state of shock. We are drawn to the light yet we cannot rest because we still think of what could have been here on this earth plane. This young soldier wanted to say "good bye" and that she should live for herself and the rest of the family now he is safe in the hands of 'God'. This is the best we can do for our loved ones that pass this way. I am not saying that his wife should go look for another husband but that she does need closure of how he passed.

Our young men and women in the Armed Forces are fighting for our freedom and right to live the way we choose, as well as actually defending the rights of their own love ones. They know that if tyranny spreads they would have given up their lives in vain. This soldier's widow never came to speak to her husband but this soldier is resting in peace now because he was allowed to say his piece.

This happens often and the point is that someone listened. If there are any other widows or parents of young soldiers reading this book, please understand that this is only one story, yet every soldier I communicated with up until the completion of this book in 2011, feels the same way. Honor their belief in freedom, they have no need to have their soul prayed for, they are already sitting at the right hand of the Almighty.

# Chapter 9
## Angela

LYNN: Angela is a young woman in her twenties who lost her mother at a young age. She has a brother and father but no other women she felt close to like her mother. I was introduced to Angela by my step son Jason who in his hidden wisdom, feeling she was in need of a "reading"

Angela: "I did expect my mother to come through and that she would let me know that she was there, that is what happened! With very definite description of herself and certain information that made me know it was her. I was not sure what my mother would reveal or to what extent she would discuss the information. I was trying to get direction from my mother and was interested to see if she would make contact in the session and wondered what she would say. I was pleased with the result of my reading with you. My mom came through and told me that she was proud of me and she was still with me. She gave me more confidence in my belief that she was with me when I needed her. Some of the information that came out in the reading made me feel a lot better about some of the decisions I had made and was about to make."

"In part of my reading you had said that something important was going to be happening to me, in the spring that would be very important to me around the anniversary of my mother's passing…something did happen that was life-changing for me. I was accepted into a graduate program."

"There was also information about people in my family that turned out to be very interesting and on point. There were messages for my dad and brother from my mom and it was like her kind-of talking to them through you. These things were very significant to me. She also said something about speaking what I was truly feeling. Because of this reading and the information I received from my mother through you I feel a great deal of support from her and know that she is always with me."

It was like a breath of fresh air. I remember saying, after I had my first reading that it had been a year and a half since I talked to my mother but that day changed it and for the first time since she died I felt I had talked with her."

That day, after the reading with you Lynn, I felt an overwhelming happiness and comfort. The reading with you gave me a burst of energy; a revitalization that I can't explain. It was overwhelming, in a beneficial way."

LYNN: Angela is moving on with her life and has had other readings with confirmation that her mother is still guiding her in her life. Angela is a wonderful young woman that always has a smile. Angela, through her readings, was able to continue her education and grow as mom watches her from the Spirit side. She still misses her mom terribly yet understands that her mother is still with her in times of need.

# Chapter 10
# Kelly

LYNN: "Kelly is a young woman from Pawtucket, Rhode Island who took care of her mom for quite some time before her mother made her transition to Spirit. Kelly always felt she needed some closure because of what her mom went through medically in the last years of her life. Kelly has had 2 readings with me, both at parties at her Aunt Cathy's home.

Kelly: "The first time you gave me a reading my Aunt Kathy's, you sat on the couch just like my mother and you preceded to prop up pillows in the exact same way. I just knew she was there and I really needed that. It was exactly like her, it was unbelievable! It gave me such a sense of peace that her Spirit was still alive. You sat on the couch and told me you had to get comfortable that you had a pain in your back; it was in the same place my mother use to get it.

LYNN: In many cases Spirit relatives come close enough to me and I allow them to give me certain characteristics that loved ones would remember. Kelly was very open and truly needed to communicate with her mom. Her mom knew and understood this. Many times when one has a "dying experience", they are prepared for life on the side of Spirit. Kelly's mom was ill for quite some time and during this time period, when one is sleeping or in a dazed condition or even if in an altered state due to medication, they are, at times, spending their time in the world of Spirit. It may seem like a dream to them, they may even talk about their own parents or friends that have passed. Kelly's mom did experience this in her last few months and she was truly ready to communicate with Kelly when Kelly was ready.

LYNN: During this book interview Kelly actually came prepared with a written statement. Here is what she had to say:

Kelly: "I took care of my mother and one of the first things she came through with was she said that she had a hard time watching me take care of her because I had given up much of my own life to do so. She also asked if I enjoyed taking care of her. It seemed like she really needed to know that. My dad also came through in a similar way. He had pain in his back and you also said that you felt like you had oxygen on your face and my father actually wore an oxygen mask on his face and he would actually pull it off his face and you kept making the same motion he use to do". When my father came through you said that you were having a hard time getting him to talk about what he was feeling, and that is so how my father was."

Kelly: "One of the things you told me was my mom said not to go to the cemetery any more. I had to laugh at that because I use to go to the cemetery all the time. I just talk to her all the time now. I don't feel like I have to go to the cemetery anymore, anytime I want to talk to her I know she is there. You also made a comment about my mother and father dancing again. My mom and dad use to go dancing all the time! You said so many things that were true; I honestly don't think there was anything you said that wasn't true. You also mentioned that my mother thought I was focused and have calmed downed quite a bit and I feel that myself. I am also more focused on what I want in a relationship where I may not have been 2 years ago when I first saw you".

LYNN: During Kelly's interview, I kept getting the word "electrician", I did not know why but when I mentioned it to Kelly she said her father was an electrician. So…I told her jokingly that I thought her dad was with us, and he was! Kelly mentioned that she had wanted to ask her mom and dad a few questions that she did not ask in the reading and I just had to oblige her, especially since I felt her mother and father were there that day to answer them. Kelly got her answers and is moving forward with her life and doing very well speaking to her parents whenever she needs to. Kelly has no regrets in caring for her parents or living in the house she cared for her parents in. The last time I saw her she was full of life and ready for what mom and dad were helping her plan. She also mentioned that she actually feels her mom around her.

During her reading I informed Kelly that her mother had been making herself known to her by tickling her back. This threw Kelly back because she had felt that very strongly but was not aware that it was her mother. She was made aware of what to look for when Spirit wants to let you know they are there. Kelly is much more aware now of the forces of her loved ones around her and is confident that they are at peace, growing and working their way through the Spirit World.

Update: from email
"Hi Lynn, I'm not sure if you know who I am by my name. I'm Kathy C's niece; I just wanted to share something with you. In September I had a reading with you at Kathy's and you said that I was going to have a baby. Well expecting my little boy 5 weeks from today! You also said my boyfriend would get another job and he did... You continue to amaze me every time. I am so happy that the Spirits blessed me with a child. I definitely believe they helped out and that they have watched over me throughout my pregnancy and will continue to watch over my little one and me! Hope all is well. Take care. Kelly C."

August 2011: I have since seen Kelly again with her 1-year-old baby boy. Mom, Dad and child are fantastic and Kelly feels very blessed and knows her parents are helping her help herself when needed from the Spirit Realm.

# Chapter 11
## Cheryl

Cheryl: "First you brought me my grandmother by describing her and mentioning something about 'August' the month. My grandmother, Augusta Nunes, was a 'well built women' and very loving just as you described. You talked about her not being born here and information about her life. You kept telling me she was sewing a lot, very busy. My grandmother was a very loving woman and did come from Portugal. My grandmother Augusta was a seamstress by trade when she was alive. This is she on one of her trips back to Portugal. (she brought a photo for that last interview)You also mentioned wedding gown.

LYNN: During her interview I started to ask Cheryl to describe her feelings after her brother died and after her reading with me. She never got a chance. I was feeling the anguish, distress and all other emotions related to losing a child or sibling. I stopped her answer in mid sentence. I immediately asked who passed in the last 6 months that would have all these feelings about her brother's passing 3 years ago, and who passed suddenly or unexpectedly. I just could not stop these emotions because although I was feeling very distraught at that point, I also felt joy (from the Spirit trying to come through) at Cheryl being there with me. I asked my guides for help just as Cheryl said; "My Mother, she passed in her sleep just a week before Christmas". Cheryl and I both had tears running down our cheeks, this is very unusual for me I can usually control this. Cheryl's mom Jeannie came in very strong. What she said to Cheryl was very important to the family. Jeannie also wanted Cheryl to know she was more content and a little more at peace and was pretty happy that she was able to meet up with her son, Brian, the brother that had been lost 3 years earlier.

Cheryl's mom kept mentioning June and I had the feeling of things being okay. We talked a little about birthdays in June but I did not quite fool that was what her mother was trying to say. At the end of the interview, she remembered that there was something important going on at her father's house in June.

During this 'book interview' Cheryl received some very important information from her mother about her father, still here on this earth plane. Cheryl's mom, Jeanne, seemed to have a lot to say about the family which proved correct at this point in their lives. It was also needed for Cheryl to hear these things from her mom.

After Jeannie was done, Brian, her brother in Spirit took over and had a few things to say to Cheryl himself. Although Cheryl is still having a hard time dealing with her mother's passing. It seems she was extremely happy to know the family was together.

Cheryl: "When my brother, Brain, came in he came in as boisterous as he was in life. He was very funny and you were laughing and talking about his children and child hood things he and I did years ago. Your mannerisms and type of language you were using were exactly as I remember my brother Brian using. There was so much he had to say about his children that I felt was accurate, I just could not stop the tears.

LYNN: At this point, (although it is not a normal question I usually ask in the book interview), I decided to ask Cheryl if her reading with me last year helped open her to any dreams from Brian. (Spirit communicates this way often).

Cheryl: "Just before my mother died I went to breakfast with my mother and father. The night before that breakfast I had a dream of my brother, Brian's face on a television screen, just his face, nothing else, sort of like a close up. I had never seen his face or my grandmother's in dreams before. I just knew they were in my dreams but I never saw his face. I remember telling my mother and father that I felt he was trying to tell me something. I did not know then but I believe he wanted to let me know he was there for me or for my mom when she passed, shortly after".

LYNN: My biggest belief in bringing Spirit messages to those in need is the <u>need</u>. In Cheryl's reading her mother, Jeannie, really <u>needed</u> to get her message to Cheryl. Keep in mind that Cheryl also needed what her mother came to give her.

# Chapter 12
## Ivette

LYNN: The first time I met Ivette was at the Springfield Spiritualist Church, Springfield, Massachusetts; I brought her mother to her and her father during the message part of the Spiritualist service. This is common practice at Spiritualist Churches. After that she sought me out for a private reading, both at the First Spiritualist Church of Springfield's "Mediums' Day" and for a phone reading, as she lives about 3 hours from my center.

Ivette: "I was very impressed with your description of my mother you gave to my father and me during a church service. At the next church Mediums' Day I sought you out for a personal reading. My mother came to me, Nareiva, she came to give me information about my father, which has been confirmed. He is not ready to go yet and he is being well taken care of here with me but his health is failing. My mother also let me know that she will be there waiting for him when it is his time. This gave me peace that my dad will be with my mother when it is his time".

"My mother's oldest brother came to me. You brought him to me by name, Augustine. I believe he is the man that gave the communication and information during one of the readings, Augustine Carbo".

"One of the people you brought to me was my grandmother from my father's side. You said that it was a grandmother but she was also saying godmother and very religious. I knew exactly who it was as my fraternal grandmother was also my godmother. My mother's mother also came with her. They came together. You described my mother's mother perfectly, just as I remembered her".

"During this reading I was getting ready for a trip. You started out by telling me that my mother wanted me to have a wonderful trip to Spain. I had just made the arrangements. You told me that I would have a very special time there. You also told me I would meet a special gentleman and we would have a wonderful time. You also said that he would have more interest in me than I in him. There would be something blocking our relationship. You also said it would be my decision. You were right on all counts. I was glad for that as I had no great expectations and just enjoyed my trip and the lovely places the gentleman took me".

"When I asked you about information about my son and his job you told me he would be much more at ease with another position that was coming up for him. He was with a very prestigious law firm and doing extremely well but he felt something was missing. He is working as a prosecutor now and is much happier. He is not making as much money, as you said but you also said he would be much more at ease and he is much happier and at peace now that he has more time with his beautiful family. After having many readings with you, I always feel much better and more certain about the future with the Spirits looking over me in my life".

"Information was given to me by you that there was going to be another addition to my family. Someone was going to have a baby and there would be a second baby. I could not think of who was expecting. You explained to me that this information was coming to me from my Spirit loved ones to let me know they are there. When I went to Porto Rico, my cousin, who is also the granddaughter of my grandfather, her daughter was expecting her second child. You said you were not sure if it was a boy or a girl but that the child's name was going to be part of the grandmother's or grandfather's name. The second name of that baby was the same name as my cousin who is the grandmother. The name is in a different language than Porto Rican but it is the same name".

"In one of the readings I told you I was going to Columbia for a personal reason. Spirit advised me not to go and I took their advice. I am glad I did! We never got into information about why I should not go to Columbia. It was good enough for me that my relatives in Spirit, through you, did not think I should go".

LYNN: I would like to speak a little about "free will" here. This is something that God gave to each and every one of us. Although our Spirit people will guide us, it is up to us to weigh the odds and make the decision for ourselves. In this case Ivette still wanted to follow her own mind, but did a little more investigating on the subject of her choice.

Ivette: 'Without you knowing I pursued the issue of going to Columbia and found that I could obtain what I wanted here in the States, in California. It was when I was getting ready to go to a special type of doctor in California that I had another reading from you. My mother came to you bringing in a Spirit doctor and told you to tell me that there was a doctor that would give me what I was looking for closer to where I lived and it would be easier for me to get to him. You also said that I would be very satisfied with him. You kept saying Spirit said closer, closer. Later when I received information on this subject I cancelled my appointment in California and went to a doctor in New York City. This enabled me to save money, not travel so far and yes I am very satisfied. My doctor was even featured on a television special and I know I am in good hands. If it was not for the information you gave me on this subject I would not have know about my other options. It is because of these instances, and what was happening to me at that time, I feel that this was the most dramatic part of my reading. Thank you.

"I received a phone call from you one morning that you had a dream about my mother. I had started dating a man that she wanted to warn me away from. You said you dreamt about her and had to call me. You did not know why but that you could not rest until you gave the message to me about my mother saying he was not good for me. Because of my past experiences with you I decided to test the gentleman and I did not hear from him again. About 3 months after your phone call to me I found out he had been incarcerated in the past, was on drugs, and alcoholic and had a family in another country. He had kept all this from me but my loved ones again protected me, this kept me from feeling used and allowed me to keep my dignity".

LYNN: "It is rare that other people's relatives come into my dreams but I believe because my relationship with Ivette is on a more personal level, and at the time I saw her often during church services in Springfield, her mom needed to make this information known. Many times we think we are receiving goodness when we meet someone that we have been looking for so long, we wear rose-colored glasses, Spirit is there to open our eyes if only we allow them to, as Ivette did".

# Chapter 13
## Jessica


LYNN: Jessica is from Worchester, Massachusetts and found me in a regional magazine called "Spirit of Change". Jessica had never had a reading of this sort before and was curious so she thought she would give it a try. Spirit always leads us in the right direction. It is up to us to take our lives into our hands. Jessica did when following her instinct, no matter what the reason she had thought of at the time. Jessica was one of my phone readings, which goes to prove, Spirit can communicate at any distance.

Jessica: "First you gave me the name Gertrude; I knew immediately who she was. This was not an easy name to come up with. She was a friend of mine. She told you something on the podium at your church and that she and I were like best friends." And we were!

LYNN: This was a message I received for Jessica when I was doing a service at our Spiritualist Church. This happens often when Spirit knows I am going to give a one on one reading later in the day).

"When my grandfather came in you gave me a little of what he looked like but the most important identification was that he came in saying, "Thank you, Jess for taking care of my wife when she was ill". I did take care of her in her last years before she died. He also stated he was with her in the 'Spirit World' as well as the child they had lost. How would you know they had a child in Spirit? He also stated he has been watching the lawyer. At that time I, had been in touch with legal counsel for legal/medical matters. He also had quite a bit to say about the first accident I was in and that it was he I felt around me, as I believed at the time".

LYNN: When Jessica asked more information from her grandfather and myself about the lawyer he said, "The lawyer will eventually understand what Jessica was getting at and he will go along with it". Jessica called me a couple of weeks later and told me he did!

Jessica: "After the description of my grandmother, you told me that my grandmother wanted to say 'sorry' to my mother about a disagreement she had with my mother. My grandmother was trying to get that message to my mother in her dreams. She was trying to say sorry to my mother for what she did. I believe this would be meaningful to my mother if she would allow me to talk about my deceased grandmother but my mother does not believe in this sort of thing. It is meaningful to me and maybe someday I can talk to my mother about it. (Jessica then told me her mother had mentioned at times that her mom and her grandmother did not speak for a while before her passing). My grandmother also called me 'Baby Doll' and I had not heard that in years, yet it came through you. My grandmother and grandfather mentioned many things that I knew of, or were happening in my life at the time, that you would have no way of knowing".

LYNN: In her reading, information came through for Jessica about trusting herself and the information she was receiving from me about herself especially about her allergies and feelings. Jessica is a nurse and although Spirit did not give her specific information about her allergies they were warning her through her dreams and other means about what to trust and what or who not to trust.

When I asked Jessica if her reading was what she expected she said it was beyond what she had expected. Her reading also helped her to learn to trust herself with her own messages she was receiving from the World of Spirit. Jessica admits that she has a long way to go but she is on her way. Jessica learned to work with Spirit in dealing with her own health as well as with helping others. She also said that her reading helped her realize that she was not "going crazy" when she thought she heard a voice of a love one that had passed, or footsteps that sounded like her grandfather. Jessica also stated that she does not have any more confusion with what she was feeling and hearing.

There are many people today receiving information from their loved ones in Spirit and think they are 'going crazy', 'seeing things' or are not understanding the signs that Spirit is trying to give to them. Jessica was one of these people. Since her reading she had improved her ties to the Spirit World and has learned to trust her intuition. She has learned to recognize her 'triggers', like her grandmother calling her 'baby doll' and the tone of voice her grandfather would use.

Jessica is an anxious type of person and does not relax easily therefore would have a hard time meditating without help. She has found, as I tell many of my students and clients, that she is most receptive when doing mundane or everyday activities like washing dishes, showering or taking a walk.

Since our reading we have talked several times as she has been paying attention to her own intuitiveness. Jessica said that her reading had clarified that her love ones in Spirit were trying to communicate with her for many years and the information she is receiving now is definitely clearer than before the readings.

Update Spring 2011:
For sometime "Spirit People" have been telling Jessica that she would be finding a "Soul mate" and to start packing. Well, she will now be moving soon, when she and her fiancé find their perfect home!

LYNN: "Trust" Accept the information and watch it unfold!

# Chapter 14
## Lori

LYNN: Lori is from my hometown of Bristol, Rhode Island and came to me interested in having a reading. She had found out about me from her cousin Linda. Lori has had many different types of reading in the past, including mediums, so this was nothing new for her. Lori has many relatives on the side of Spirit. Most of them came by to say hello, but Lori had been waiting for many years to hear from a special friend and had not until the day of her reading.

Lori: "Lynn, you brought through both of my grandfathers. You described my first grandfather and included the family gatherings we always had in the summer. He told you to give me the month of July, that was his birthday and this helped me make certain it was him. You also described the hat that he always wore and you did mention the garden. This is all true and it is what I remember the most. He came first. You also seemed to take on his mannerisms to the 'T'.

"There was so much detail you gave me about my grandmother and her sisters, like the kind of statue she had on her dresser. You brought one of my grandmothers to me by giving me her name in a very beautiful way. You told me you smelled roses. You said that usually that meant it was their name or they had roses in their yard, her name is Rose. Her sister came letting me know that they were together again. You described the statue of the blessed mother in the clouds and the 3 children that one you really hit on. My grandmother did have the stature of the Lady on her dresser, the Lady of Fatima. I have the same statue in my room. My cousin Linda gave it to me. I did not even know what statue it was until you told me 'the one with the clouds'.

"Then my other grandfather came to me and you really hit that one on the head, again. He came to you sitting in a wheelchair and yes, before he passed, he did need a wheelchair. You told me he was pushing the wheelchair back and forth trying to let me know he was not in the wheelchair anymore. He was free. He was throwing it off a hill and that made a lot of sense to me because he was a man that did not like to be taken care or confined. He gave me a message through you that if he knew it was so wonderful where he is, with long gone family and friends, he would have gone sooner. That is also very understandable to me and I am glad he came to give me that message. He fought and fought for a number of years before he passed and suffered some, I am glad he is at peace".

"My grandmother's sister's husband (my uncle) came. He was also in a wheelchair but you again, described him perfectly by telling me he had no legs. That is the difference between him and my grandfather and you described a clinical setting and he passed in a nursing home. My uncle, my grandmother's son was made known to me. You told me he said he likes to play tricks on people here on the earth plane from the Spirit side. He does too! Light bulbs at my aunt house always have to be changed and when they placed elsewhere they work."

"After that you described my grandmother's boyfriend, who stopped in to say hi. (This grandmother is still alive) He was a golfer and he came through in that way."

"My uncle Matt, my grandfather's other brother was described. I definitely knew it was him by you calling me "Caretha". He always called me Caretha. He was the only one". (This is a Portuguese term for dear or beautiful).

"What impressed me also about the reading were your mannerisms. When you spoke about a certain relative you would say things in the same way with the same type of definition to your voice that they had in this life. This was validating to me. I asked your advice on a gentleman I had been seeing for quite some time and my friend Donna came through. The words 'you want help from her, no way in h…. will she help you with him'. That was Donna, right to the point and in that way".

LYNN: When I asked Lori if she was satisfied with her reading this was her reply:

Lori: "First, you brought me more people with concrete and positive evidence in one reading that I have ever experienced. I have been going to mediums for years, and years and years. For the last 7 years I really wanted and needed to hear from one person. She came through you. We had this deal that if there was anything to this baloney of life after death she would come back and tell me. You described her by letting me know there was a woman, not a relative, coming close that had passed with 'woman's cancer'. Many mediums have described 'cancer' but never a specific kind, this is unsettling to me as I have felt they were fishing, everyone knows someone that has had cancer. My friend, I needed to hear from had 'woman's cancer' when she was young, many years ago. Your hands were put on your body in the exact area she had pain. That is what caused her departure from this life. As soon as she came through I recognized her. She also told me that she knew her husband has remarried and he did. She also wanted me to know that she was happy that he did, and I should be too. He needed someone to take care of him, and her children. This message in itself was extremely comforting to me. Her husband did marry again, and as far as I was concerned, married a little too soon after she had passed. I carried that around as guilt with me for quite some time."

"As I listen to you speak, I felt she was right there in the room and I felt differently about him marring again when you gave me the words, 'he needed someone to take care of him'. I knew she was at peace. She also told you that she was watching over her grandchildren, she does have grandchildren now. This too confirmed that it was Donna, who I wanted to speak to for so long. There is no way you would have known any of her information. I am so happy she came to me that day. She never did in the past. Through you I understand much more of the Spirit World".

"We were very close and worked together, just her and me during her illness. She lost so much weight and needed to be built up. I do not know how many pounds I put on trying to help her keep her strength up. She always treated me like one of her kids and you pinpointed it when you said, 'I was like one of her little ducklings'. She was the one I always wanted to hear from".

# Chapter 15
# Mary

LYNN: Mary is from Westborough, Massachusetts; her reading was a gift from a mutual friend. She wanted to connect to her sister on the side of Spirit. Mary came to see me in the fall and came back about 6 months later. Although I did not know when she came the first time she had a specific reason for it, I found out later when giving her a message and it came through loud and clear.

In Mary's first reading, her sister came to her by having me describing her illness and it seems that although Mary wanted to hear from her sister, it seems her sister had ideas of her own in wanting to come to speak to Mary. Hearing from her sister and the identification she used were very meaningful to Mary. There is also specific information that Mary's sister gave her about Mary's niece, the daughter of this woman on the side of Spirit. During the reading Mary's sister told her this daughter, now in college, would be making a drastic change to her curriculum and that it was okay with her mother (Mary's sister).

Two days after Mary's reading she spoke to her niece. Her niece had been planning to go to Europe as part of her education but had now made certain changes in her curriculum and would not be going to Europe in January after all. It was a big decision for this young girl. Mary was very surprised because her niece had been planning this for quite some time.

LYNN: Sometimes Spirit will give information about a loved one to let you know they are with you and still care and want to be there to help. This may happen in many different ways and when Mary's sister told her about helping her own daughter and this information was confirmed 2 days later, Mary and her niece truly knew 'Spirit still lives'.

In Mary's second reading about 6 months after the first, the same type of thing happened and Mary confirmed all and we decided to do the 'book interview' directly after her second reading.

Ben, Mary's former husband came through very strong. Ben gave me certain information that I would not have known, some of a personal nature and information like him riding his motorcycle and revving the motor. He also spoke about the dog he left behind and living near the railroad track when they were first married. Ben had also stated directly that he needed to get information to a young woman, his daughter, that he was alright and she needs to 'be happy', Mary stated, All these things you mentioned, along with his personality were definitely Ben.

Mary: "I had lunch with my youngest daughter just before coming to see you today and she is still very upset and is having a hard time dealing with his death".

LYNN: Mary was also concerned with a waiting period that a deceased person may need to experience before coming to greet someone here on the earth plane. Mary was concerned because her former husband had only been on the side of Spirit for 6 months. In my experience, Spirit may make their way from time of death to 20+ years later.

LYNN: A person that has crossed may come back immediately to give information that is needed or to give a loving message to someone that is still here. In Mary's case it is her daughter, who was with her father when he passed. Sometimes people feel they could have done more, but we must realize it is not for us to say.

Elderly people or those who were ill for some time would have an easy crossing; their Spirit body would have been prepared ahead of time. They were prepared to enter the World of Spirit and therefore have an easier time coming through to a medium.

Those that have experienced a 'sudden death' like a heart attack or accident may be a little confused upon entering the "Spirit World" and not be able to make contact immediately. These souls are not lost, just confused for a while, because their loved ones are not speaking or seeing them anymore. Some of these Spirit people realize this by the day of their funeral, for some it takes many, many years. For some Spirits those that still live on this plane, mourning for them, cannot let them go or have pangs of unwarranted guilt. If our grieving goes on too long, in a negative way, they cannot move forward within the Spirit World. We must understand our Spirit loved ones who watch us suffer unwarranted guilt get depressed themselves just as they would on earth. Moving on in our own life, no matter how miserable we think we are, is the best thing we can do for them as well as ourselves. Do something to remember them by or help in a volunteering way. Something they will be proud of, it will also keep you busy. If you work be happy and offer up your love to them during the working day as if they are sitting next to you, after all they very well may be!

My experience with suicides has taught me that they are truly sorry for the hurt they have caused their loved ones here on the earth plane. To truly grow on the side of Spirit, I am told that they must willingly help those they have left behind. I have not experienced any soul or Spirit that did not want to make up for the hurt and guilt they have left their family and friends with. Many times what they thought was bothering them when, they were here, was trivial to what they see their loved ones dealing with here on the Earth Plane. All it takes is to ask for their help and forgiveness or give it to them your forgiveness if that be the case.

So you now understand some of the ways or reasons why Spirit will or will not come back to give information to a loved one right away.

Ben needed and wanted to assure his daughter that she should not have any guilt about his passing. Ben was strong that day and he understood his former wife's concern immensely. Later in the year a young girl came to me for a reading, unknowingly it was Mary's daughter and 'Ben', came to speak, in person, to his daughter who was the first person who found him after he had crossed to the Spirit World.

# Chapter 16
# Tanya

Tanya: "The last time I saw you I had this simply wonderful experience that I will share with you now. I know you knew a little bit about my experience because I understand that our mutual friend, Linda, told you about it. I was not going to call you but I had this very intense dream about you, on March 7<sup>th</sup> and I woke up from the dream and I knew I just had to call you".

LYNN: Spirit does get the message through when they want to, sometimes in dreams sometimes by sending an Angel in disguise.

Tanya: "When I listened to my tapes there were 2 specific things that were very meaningful to me. First you spoke about my great-maternal-grandmother, who I really did not have any information on whatsoever. BUT... my Nana's daughter is unfortunately dying and was at Nana's house for Easter and she started telling me about her mother and how she was a great baker, and they were so poor and she use to bake this bread and make a lot of soup because it went a long way. In my reading you spoke about this woman who you identified as my mother's grandmother and you saw her with a full apron on and she was baking bread and making the soup. You also said that she had to do this for a lot of people even though she did not have a lot. Her message was that I was doing a good job of taking care of the outside of myself but I was not doing such a good job with the inside. On Easter Sunday, all my grandmother did was talk about her mother. It was not until last Saturday that I listened to my tape and I just could not believe how this information came to me, I just said 'Holy Molly'. I guess I need to look at my inside too!"

"We also spoke about my friend Larry. It was kind of hard to communicate with Larry; you had said that someone or something was

67

holding him back, probably someone here on the earth plane, someone that may be still feeling guilt ridden or grieving. As you went on, he told you; nobody understood your relationship. "I did not tell you the intensity of our relationship. Then you said: 'Is there a chance that if he were still here that you would have been married?' You started to come out with more and more personal things that you could have not possibly have known. You then told me that I needed to let him move on so I could also move more freely with the relationship at hand. Put away the feelings you had been carrying of 'what ifs'. You told me, "let go of the past and that he will be sending me a sign that he was ready to move on, yet still guiding me as a friend".

"Now, my intention was to go back to work when I left your office because it was early enough, about 2:30 pm. I had such an emotional reaction to our conversation, I was overwhelmed and needed to be alone, so I went home. I got home and the phone rang, it was the 'tile man'. We had a leak in our shower and needed to have it repaired and retiled. We did not know anyone so my husband had found this 'tile guy' in the phone book, he just happened to call at a time that I should not have been home, but I was. He found a tile that he thought would match, and would I mind if he dropped it off. I told him my husband was not home, because that is whom he had been dealing with. He said, 'That is okay, I just want to drop it off'. I was really kind of annoyed; I just wanted peace and quiet in my own home. I even felt a little MAD! I was a little uncomfortable being alone with a strange man in my house, while in the bathroom he said, 'While I am here would you mind if I write out the invoice?' I said: No, go ahead. He said: 'Can I do it at your kitchen table; it would just be a little easier?' We walked down the stairs, my husband is Jewish I am Catholic, so we have Catholic Crosses and Star's of David all over the house. He said: 'Oh who is Jewish?' 'My husband is Jewish and I am Catholic', I said. He said, 'Oh it is really hard, isn't it?' I said, 'No not for us.' We seem to be able to blend the best of both".

"Oh my son is married to a Jewish girl and is getting divorced and I think it is because of the religion, how do you make it work? The 'tile guy' questioned."

"I told him we always include each other's faiths and are respectful of each other and our beliefs".

"How did you and your husband meet"?

"We knew each other since high school in Providence, although I grew up on Federal Hill and my husband grew up on the East Side, we did not date then but we have known each other for quite some time".

He said: "Oh I did so much tile work on the East Side, I worked for a good friend of mine, (this name will remain privileged), and you could have knocked me over, that was Larry's father! "Lynn this is, I know sent by Larry's Spirit, my husband just looked up tile services in the phone book. What are the chances? What other chances are there that I would be home"? You had told me that this month was important; I had said that it was the anniversary of Larry's passing. You said he was planning something or doing something important around his 'birthday into Spirit' as you called it. It was not so much the reading that was of importance, it was what happened afterwards".

"I told him I knew the family and I went to high school with their son, the one that died."

He said: "Yeah, I remember so many years ago how that boy suffered and the heartbreak of his parents, my wife and I lit so many candles for them. When I use to work with his father, a "Tile Man", I remember him saying how his son was in love with a girl who wasn't Jewish."

I said, "I know today is the anniversary of his death". It was awful. Lynn: My heart was crumbling. It would break my friend's heart, because he knew how much his son cared for this girl who was not Jewish. He even told me that if any of his kids or my kids wanted to get married he could never allow it, because we were not Jewish. It used to break his heart, because he and his wife thought this girl was a real nice girl and cared for their son deeply. All these years, since I was 14 years old, I thought it was because I came from a poor family and a poor neighborhood and not my religion, which keep me from him and his family.

I said, "I was that girl"!

"Wow, what a small world" the "Tile Man" said.

"You know I never realized that his family had an opinion of me, one way or the other", I told him. He completed his business and my husband came home about 3 minutes later, if my husband was home and if I did not arrive home early, this conversation would not have happened. I could not wait to tell my husband my story. Thank you Lynn for helping Larry send me the truth".

LYNN: Tanya stated that this was such a gift for her especially that night. To realize that it had nothing to do with her as a person from a poorer area of town than Larry was. (This couple was separated at an early age; I can't help but wonder if the parents would have changed their mind if they knew that their son would not be long in this world. Would they have agreed just to see him happy?) Tanya now has more confidence in herself as well; she is also able to dedicate herself in a more stunning way to her husband, children and their future. The message her great-grandmother gave her about taking care of the inside as well as the outside did happen with the help of Spirit. She comes once in a while for meditations to keep her centered and finds herself more organized. Tanya's reading was very powerful, as she told me, but she also realized that she understood her own powerful gifts from Larry as he sent her a very distinct message and was every bit as meaningful for her on many levels. This is the ultimate in Synchronicity!

# Chapter 17
## Eric's Story

I have saved this story for the last because it is very special and meaningful. It is meant to be a tribute to this child, his family and to all children who now live with the "Angels".

LYNN: Donna came to me through very unusual circumstances; she and her family are from Middletown, Rhode Island. In a previous story I had mentioned that when Spirit wants to contact a loved one they will use any means within Universal Law to contact them. Please note that Donna did not know much about mediums or that there was someone like me so close to her. Here is Eric's story, in his mother's words.

Donna: "A woman came to see you in July. All the children call her 'Miss Bettie'. Miss Bettie heard about you and came to contact her mother-in-law for her daughter, who had been having a hard time with the loss of her grandmother. Her mother-in-law came through very strongly; she had a belief in a life after death. (This I have found helps Spirit to communicate in a shorter amount of time than if they did not believe in life after death). Miss Betty's daughter said your mannerisms were so much like her grandmother's that she just knew you were in contact with this wonderful lady she loved so much. You got into a sitting position with your elbows on your knees (not normal for me) and this is how her grandmother sat when she talked. The young girl's friend was going to be next but you immediately said, 'No, your mother has to go next'. Your grandmother wants to speak to your mother. Miss Betty's and her daughter had a very wonderful reading with you and my friend is more at peace about her grandmother's death".

"Miss Betty came in and her mother-in-law was cradling a baby, like caring for it at this moment. You told her a baby, a toddler had come to see her and Betty was not recognizing who it could be. Betty said that it could be a child her mother–in–law lost in a miscarriage years ago but you said that it was one that did make it to life but not for long, this child was very young like 2, a toddler. You kept saying that the child was trying to get through and it sounded like an 'E' name. His name is Eric you said. Her mother-in-law passed 2 months after my son Eric, Donna stated. This mother–in –law of Betty's knew of Eric and his passing and illness and would say things to Betty like why this child why not me. (Her husband had passed the year before, she was ready and of an age to welcome an easy passing).

"Lynn, you had told Miss Betty that it was a toddler age 2 a boy just learning how to talk. He passed in the hospital with a blood disease or cancer. He passed on a special day, not a noted holiday like Christmas or Easter but a special day. MY son Eric passed on Valentine's Day 2004. You told her he was a very cuddly little boy and was cuddling with her. Miss Betty was still thinking family or very close friends and could not recognize this little angel. You kept saying the child had an 'E' name and that the father's name had something unusual like a 'By…' in it. My husband's name is Byron, not a common name today. The child was nodding his head like whatever Miss Betty was thinking was right on. It was at this time that Miss Betty realized who he might be. The child, Eric was worried about his parents. (Miss Betty baby-sits for Eric's cousin, Kyle). He wanted his parents to know that he had an easy crossing and was not afraid when he crossed to Spirit. He was concerned about his parents; he misses mommy and playtime with his sisters. Eric did not stop there; he kept giving you confirmation that it was he trying to contact his mommy. He told you, Lynn, he had new friends and was playing again".

"A most important thing to me was that you said he was humming and doing something with his hands. You then said he was singing 'Itsy, Bitsy, Spider' and doing it with his hands. Kristen and Miss Betty do not know this but 'Itsy Bitsy Spider' was the first song Eric learned and he always sang it"

"You also said he is okay, no hurt! Just in that way. Eric also told you to tell his mommy not to worry about going to the cemetery anymore. How would you even begin to imagine that I always worried about the cemetery and Eric's grave? That particular day I was crazy because I forgot to buy flowers at S&S. I was always worried about keeping the grave looking nice on a daily basis. That day Miss Betty tells me this, I just had to stop and realize my baby was with me".

"Previous to that my therapist had given me a book about a medium. I read it the night before Miss Betty called me. Prior to that I believe I would not have been so open to what she had said. I never knew anything about mediums. I felt it just put me in the right place to accept Eric's message. My therapist said she was not going to give it to me but this woman came in her office that morning and saw it on the table, she communicates with Angels. She said: 'Oh you want to give that to someone but you are not sure, she needs to read it'. That is how I happened to have it and read it that night".

Lynn: I call this synchronicity; there are no coincidences where Spirit is concerned.

Donna: "The next morning I spoke to my mother, she was on her way into the hospital for a biopsy. We spoke about the book and I told her that I was truly starting to believe that 'they', our love ones in Spirit, are really with us. I told my mother that I spoke to Eric and ask him to go with her and help her get through this. Later when my mother returned home she said; 'Oh Donna, I really think he was there because at the time of the biopsy I was praying and thought, I wish I knew someone there because I felt so alone and suddenly here comes my cousin, she worked there and I did not expect to see her or anyone I knew'.

LYNN: Donna is an engineer and people that live in a fact and figures world sometimes have a harder time accepting that Spirit is with them. Spirit knew this and prepared Donna ahead of time for her to open to Spirit messages. All this synchronicity that Spirit put in place for

Donna happened prior to her phone call from Kristen and Miss Betty. Donna does believe that Spirit but these happenings In her path so she would be more accepting of her son Eric's message: First the book - then the happening with her mom - then Miss Betty's experience with Eric. Higher energies, guides, the Angels and Eric planned all this for Donna ahead of time, so by the time she came to see me she was open and ready to speak to her baby, Eric.

LYNN: Up to this point, this was all information that was given to a friend of a relative of Eric's mom. Donna's sister-in-law called her immediately so she could speak with Betty and learn. The rest is Eric's history in Spirit. I find that many times Spirit will utilize the people you least expect to hear from, like a friend of the family. They are usually willing candidates although they may not be aware that they are a catalyst for Spirit.

Donna: "Lynn, it was about a month after I spoke to Miss Betty that I came to see you, I did not let you know who I was yet Eric came through very strong along with my grandparents who were caring for my son in the Spirit World. You said my grandmother was taking better care of him than she did of me and she took great care of me so that was very comforting and I understood it completely".

"My grandparents came first, my grandmother in a very significant way, along with her description, you smelled roses, my grandmother's middle name was Rose and I named my daughter Victoria Rose after her. You also brought my aunt in with my grandmother and said that my grandmother was glad to be reunited with her child. My mother's sister passed when she was two. This was significant as my grandmother passed at 92 and always spoke about the child she had lost. My maternal grandmother was always with us, she loved babies and children it gave me great comfort that she was with my son".

Lynn: Donna and her grandmother both lost children of the same age, and Donna is close to the age her grandmother was when she lost her daughter, Jackie. My belief is that this wonderful woman came in to give Donna strength and understanding at this time, Spirit does work in this way, with love and understanding.

Donna: "At one point in the reading you told me multiple generations of my father's side of the family were coming in, you tasted homemade wine; you knew it was homemade because you did not like it. At the time I could not think of whom it could be and I thought you were way off base. You told me you could see the grapes in their yard and this relative would have made wine at home. I later found out that my great grandparents had grapes in their yard and made wine in the cellar of the house, when they lived in Providence".

"Then it seemed to be Eric's turn. You then asked if there was a child in Spirit, I said yes, my son. You said he was sort of shy at first, Eric was! You also told me that my Italian grandmother was sort of pushing him, and yes she would be the one to push, gently but it would be her. This made me laugh and relax more also. It was so typical of both of them".

"Lynn you were so caring and understanding when you told me that before his passing he had something in his throat, that yours was irritated. You said that you (Eric) could hear everything but he could not see. It was almost as if you were in his room, especially when you mentioned wiggling. . . Eric had a tube in his throat and was on a respirator and the doctors had him paralyzed. I always talked to him even though I didn't think he could hear me. I played 'The Wiggles' and constantly spoke to him and sang to him. That information confirmed what, as a mother, I felt that what I was doing was helping Eric in some way".

"You also told me that he was very comfortable passing, 'once I let him go'. There was a time that I had to 'let him go'. I had to make the decision to turn off the machine. They told me I had the choice of this large vibrating respirator that would give him 8 hours or utilize a smaller one that would be more comfortable and I would be able to hold him but he would pass a little sooner. I chose to hold my son for hia remaining hours I could almost feel him passing easily". (I believe Eric had an easy time passing not only because of his age but his young Spirit felt his mommy gave him permission.)

"In my reading you had asked me if one of my children was seeing or talking to Eric. You said that Eric was still with someone in the family, a child. I told you no, at the time but my nephew, Kyle, was. Kyle would talk about Eric going on the bus with him; Eric would talk or play with him. A week after the funeral when Kyle was on the changing table he started laughing hysterically while looking at the crib. When his mom asked him why he was laughing, he said 'Ebic' was in the crib and was being silly. That was the first time Kyle saw Eric and every once in a while Kyle will say he sees 'Ebic', as he called him. They were very close and at this point, you gave me information about children under 5 being more open to Spirit energies, because they really have not been told otherwise".

"The other thing you told me was that he was patting his head and smiling. He showed you a short woman in front of a garage patting her head and said that he liked it 'sunny' better. My sister-in-law, Kyle's mother is very short about 4'10'' and she had just dyed her hair dark, it use to be blonde. I believe he was trying to tell her that he likes her as a blonde better".

"The day you gave me my reading my sister-in-law Kristen, Kyle's mother came with me. Eric came to her with crayons and he was coloring. (She was a little confused because Eric hadn't been coloring before he passed). Then you said that Eric was helping her son with his coloring. Kyle had some fine motor skill issues and was learning how to color, at that point we understood more about Eric helping Kyle, they are the same age and were very close and played together often".

LYNN: As a Spiritualist I do not specifically believe in reincarnation, as there is not enough proof. I just deliver the information that Spirit wishes me to. In some instances, as this with Donna, the Spirit of her son Eric told me that he wanted to come back to be near the family he loved so much. It is my understanding in dealing with this information that a piece of their essence, as I call it, will be reborn to this earth plane to be close to the loved ones. This usually happens sometime after the passing of a love one. Many times a relative, or friend through a pregnancy or adoption, will find some way for a part of them to stay near the family. This is the information that I gave Donna and what she had to tell me now, 7 months later.

Donna: "My brother's wife was pregnant at the time of my reading, she has had her baby and they named him Nicholas Eric. This seems so ironic to me because when he was born he was tiny, like Eric was, he had some issues, like Eric did, and he gave us a little scare before he was born, he had some head issues, but he is fine. I keep looking at him and going "are you Eric"? (Donna laughs) Have you seen Eric, recently?

LYNN: At this point I explain to Donna that as this new child grows to his 2$^{nd}$ year, she should look for the habits that remind her of Eric. Eric was only here on this earth plane for a very short time but those close to him will still recognize habits that he developed. That is the only way you can tell when a piece of a love one returns to us. It is easier to recognize the habits we remember of older loved ones when they decide and are given permission to return. I have also found that toddlers, as they are learning to speak, will possibly come out with a two or three word 'saying' the deceased loved one may have used often.

Donna still had more to say about a prediction I had made for her. I decided to leave that for another time, as I believe it is still in the making. I also feel this is Eric's story and we would both like to leave it this way. God Bless this wonderful little boy who is trying to teach us through his LOVE!

# Part Three
# Quick Outline on Spiritualism

Most people I come in contact with have not even heard of

"Spiritualism"

Or the meaning of many of the terms connected with

"Spirit"

www.nsac.org

Will give you a listing of Spiritualist Churches

in your area and help with understanding the spirit communication

process.

# Chapter 18
# Spiritualism

To give you some information about Spiritualism it is important for you to understand what Spiritualism is based on and the '9 Principles" we live by. They are simple and to the point and most can be found in other religions of the world. The following information is taken directly from the NSAC Spiritualist Manual.

Spiritualism is the Science, Philosophy and Religion of continuous life, based upon the demonstrated fact of communication, by means of Mediumship, with those who live in the Spirit World.

"Spiritualism is a Science" because it investigates, analyzes and classifies facts and manifestations demonstrated from the Spirit side of life.

"Spiritualism is a Philosophy" because it studies the laws of nature both on the seen and unseen sides of life and bases its conclusions upon present observed facts. It accepts statements of observed facts of past ages and conclusions drawn there from, when stained by reason and by results of observed facts of the present day.

"Spiritualism is a Religion" because it strives to understand and to comply with the Physical, Mental and Spiritual Laws of Nature "which are the Laws of God."

A Spiritualist is one who believes, as the basis of his or her religion, in the communication between this and the Spirit World by means of mediumship, and who endeavors to mold his or her character and conduct in accordance with the highest teachings derived from such communion.

A Medium is one who organism is sensitive to vibrations from the Spirit World and through whose instrumentality intelligences In that word are able to convey messages and produce the phenomena of Spiritualism.

A Spiritualist Healer is one who, either through his own inherent powers or through his or her Mediumship is able to impart vital, curative force to pathologic conditions.

# Declaration of Principles

1. We believe in Infinite Intelligence.

2. WE believe that the phenomena of Nature, both physical and spiritual, are the expression of Infinite Intelligence.

3. WE affirm that the correct understanding of such expression and living in accordance therewith constitute true religion.

4. We affirm that the existence and personal identity of the individual continue after the change call death.

5. We affirm that communication with the so-called dead is a fact, scientifically proven by the phenomena of Spiritualism.

6. We believe that the highest morality is contained in the Golden Rule: "Do unto others as you would have them do unto you."

7. We affirm the moral responsibility of individuals and that we make our own happiness or unhappiness as we obey or disobey Nature's physical and spiritual laws.

8. We affirm that the doorway to reformation is never closed against any soul here or hereafter.

9. We affirm that the precepts of Prophecy and Healing are Devine attributes proven through Mediumship.

# Declaration of Principles - simplified version
(Form for children)

1. We believe in God.

2. We believe that God is expressed through all Nature.

3. True religion is living in obedience to Nature's Law. (God's Law)

4. We never die.

5. Spiritualism proves that we can talk with people in the Spirit World.

6. Be kind, do good, and others will do likewise.

7. WE bring unhappiness to ourselves by the errors we make and we will be happy if we obey the Laws of Life. (God's Law)

8. Every day is a new beginning

9. Prophecy and healing are expressions of God.

# Hints for a Good Reading

Although there are only a few, I have found that those who follow these simple "hints" get better information from their loved ones on the Spirit side of life. That is one of the reasons I have chosen to do readings by appointment as well as having a personal life that is extremely full.

First: Relax and put your mind at ease before the reading. This creates a better atmosphere for the reading and makes it easier for Spirit to make contact.

Second: Spirit provides evidence of identity in many different ways. It can be by relationship, description of self, description of incidents, name. Be willing to verify such evidential information so the medium can proceed to the message(s) that needs to be given, if any. Many of my clients contact me later with confirmation of the person or information given at the sitting, but not immediately recognized.

Third: Contact with a specific person is not guaranteed although many people read are pleasantly surprised. However, I do suggest that you think about the person(s) that you wish to contact before your reading and make an appointment with them. It also helps when one brings a photo of the person(s) you wish to contact, one photo per envelope. It should not be shown to the medium until after the reading as description is part of identification and the Spirit person may wish to come through identifying himself or herself as they are in that specific photo. A piece of jewelry such as a ring watch bracelet or keys are also very strong contact items if a Spirit person is having a hard time connecting or the medium needs a little help.

Fourth: Something may make more sense by the end of the reading, or the understanding of the message or description may come at a later timo, after you have had a chance to think about it. So it is important NOT to be quick to say "no" to what is given.

Fifth: Many people just want to know their relatives and love ones are doing well on the Spirit Side but there are many that have specific questions for certain Spirit people. I always advise thinking about them or writing them down ahead of time. Many times the questions are answered before asked out loud and at times they have to be verbalized. No Spirit claims to have an answer on the spur of the moment. Remember they are people, in a different form, but still people. A consciousness that is NOT "all knowing", but still a little more knowledgeable than we are here on earth about our own timeline and needs. The questions should be on a personal nature of self or of them. Questions should not be asked of a Spirit person that they may have no understanding of. Such as asking a person who may have dropped out of school a question pertaining to one a lawyer may need to answer. Spirit also has the "option" of answering the question. They may not want to for their own reasons. Although those on the Spirit Side may "see" a little further into the future than we can, they are not "all knowing" and we do have "FREE WILL". Anything predicted may be changed according to your own will.

Remember we are all spiritual Beings having Human Experiences therefore it is natural to continue as Spirit.

# EPILOGUE

It is important for you to understand that all mediums work in a different way. Although you may find a favorite in the future, do not compare one to another. I do suggest going to someone that is recommended by someone you know or associated with a Spiritualist Church, as most of my clients have found me that way, I have had very little need for advertising, hence keeping my prices low. Look for one that proves the continuity of life, not just a "psychic" if your need is to communicate with loved ones.

Just because some mediums charge a lot of money does not mean they can communicate with Spirit better than a medium giving you communication in a Spiritualist Church Service for no pay. Spiritualist Churches worldwide have many good mediums that you have never heard of because most people do not know or understand what Spiritualism is. Most of us give our services free at Church services or for very little compensation, this is the same for a "Medium's Day" event. It is part of what we do. Living with and for Spirit is what we believe in. Improving our own lives and the lives of those we meet is important to us. When we promote your growth, spiritually and physically it promotes growth in ourselves. I for one believe we should always strive to connect to the Source of Creation in any way we can and whenever we can for ourselves and those around us.

Good readings also depend on YOUR attitude or openness to communicate with your love ones. Visit a medium with an open mind and no expectations. You will receive more. It is like being on "candid camera", when you least expect it the best most wonderful thing will be given to you.

Hopefully, you now have a better understanding of what Spiritualism and life after death is and trust those you trusted in your life when they were here in body that are now trying to guide you from the Spirit side of Life.

All my readings are conducted in a well-lit area; any you receive should be also. I say an invocation or prayer asking for the highest and the best for each person I read. The information in the previous pages concerning my clients is just a little of the thousands of people I have come in contact with. I wish all who purchase and read this book a life full of wonderment and prosperity from Spirit. May the Blessings of your Loved Ones be with you!

With gratitude,
Linda (Lynn) Kent

CPSIA information can be obtained at www.ICGtesting.com
Printed in the USA
BVOW032137051111

275270BV00001B/80/P